Contents

New words

claw

hatch

hide

hunt
(verb)

insect

jaw

laugh
(verb)

quiet
(adjective)

sneeze
(verb)

throat

Who makes sounds?

You hear sounds.
People make sounds.
Animals make
sounds, too.

Birds sing.

Lions roar.

Snakes hiss.

THINK!

What sounds do people make?

What do animals say?

Animals say,
"We want food!"

The baby birds make noises. Their mother gives them food.

Animals say, "Help me!"

The meerkat sees a snake. The meerkat makes a noise. Its friends run and help!

The wolf is howling. It is finding its friends.

▶ **WATCH!**

Watch the video (see page 32).
What does the meerkat do when it sees the snake?

9

How do animals make sounds?

Sounds come from parts of an animal's body.

Lions and tigers make sounds in their **throats**. The sounds come out of their mouths.

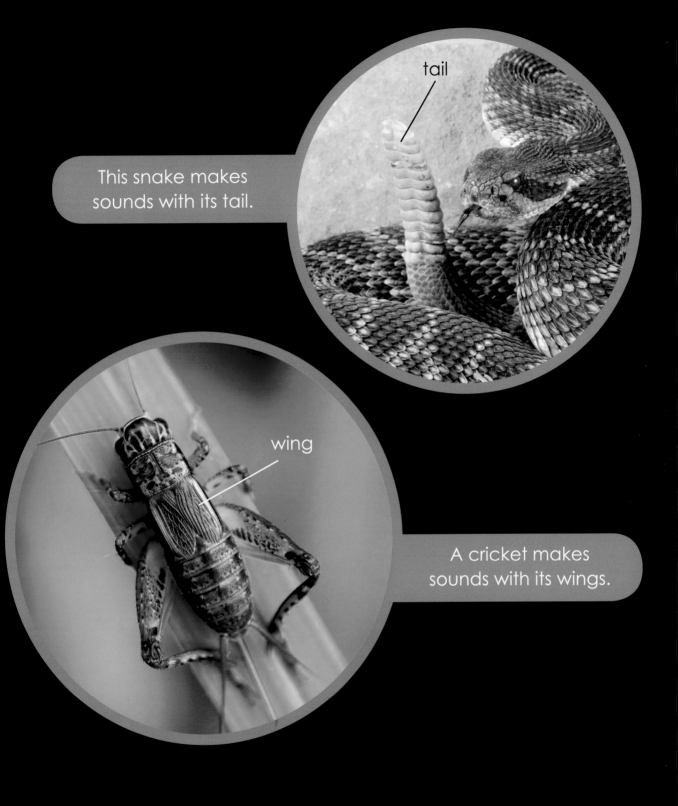

This snake makes sounds with its tail.

tail

wing

A cricket makes sounds with its wings.

THINK!

Make an animal sound. Can your friend guess what animal it is? Take turns.

Do animals sing?

Whales sing
under the sea.

Gibbons and frogs sing, too.

The family of gibbons sings, "This is our tree."

This frog sings. Other frogs come.

THINK!

When do you sing and why?

Do birds sing to their eggs?

This bird sings to her eggs.

The baby birds in the eggs hear their mother.

The baby birds are **hatching**.

The baby birds are hungry.
They are singing for food.

The mother bird is giving
food to the baby birds.

LOOK!

Look at the pages.
When does the mother bird sing to the baby birds?
When does the mother bird give food to the baby birds?

What noises do African wild dogs make?

African wild dogs live with their friends and family.

African wild dogs make a noise because they are hungry.
They **sneeze**.

This dog is hungry. It is sneezing.

The other dogs are hungry, too. They are sneezing, too. They are looking for food.

▶ **WATCH!**

Watch the video (see page 32).
These wild dogs are hungry. How do they catch the animal they want to eat?

How do animals make sounds under the water?

Some animals make
sounds under
the water.

They make sounds
with their bodies.

Whales make lots of sounds.

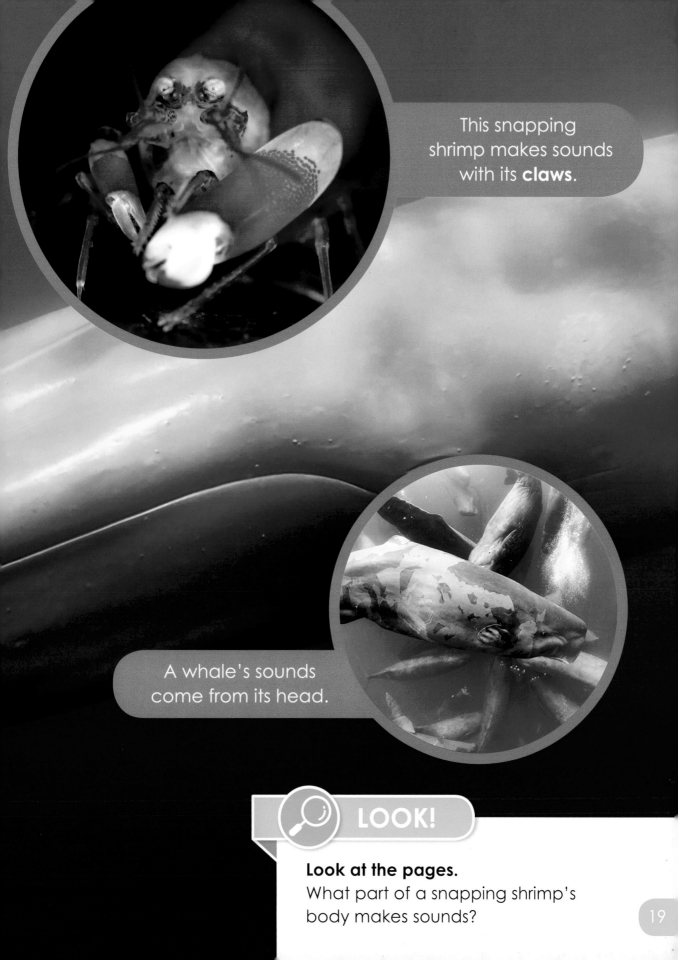

This snapping shrimp makes sounds with its **claws**.

A whale's sounds come from its head.

LOOK!

Look at the pages.
What part of a snapping shrimp's body makes sounds?

Which animals make a lot of noise?

Some animals make a lot of noise. Their friends and family hear.

Elephant seals roar from their big noses.

Howler monkeys howl.

A blue whale makes a lot of noise. It sings. More whales hear and sing, too.

FIND OUT!

How can you make a loud sound without shouting?
Cup your hands around your mouth.
Try to talk to a friend who is far away.

Which animals are quiet?

Some animals don't make many sounds. They are **quiet**.

This baby antelope is quiet. It **hides** and waits for its mother.

Owls are quiet, too. This helps owls to catch animals.

Owls can fly very quietly.

THINK!

Which other animals are quiet? Why are they quiet?

Do animals laugh?

Some animals **laugh** and play.

These baby bonobos are playing and laughing.

Chimpanzees laugh with family and friends.

WATCH!

Watch the video (see page 32).
What is the baby bonobo doing?
What is its mother doing?

How do animals hear?

Many animals hear sounds with their ears.

This sea lion has small ears.

This goat has big ears.

A dolphin does not hear with its ears. It hears with its **jaw**.

An elephant hears with its big ears.

PROJECT

Work in a group.
Find pictures of a cow, a giraffe, a chimpanzee, a cheetah and a mouse. Glue the pictures on paper, and label the animals' ears. How are the ears the same? How are they different?

HOW do bats find food with sound?

Bats fly. They **hunt insects** at night. They see at night with sound.

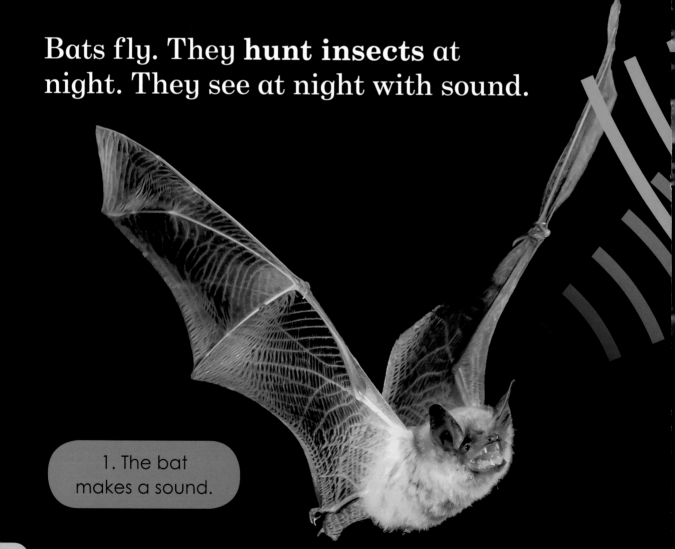

1. The bat makes a sound.

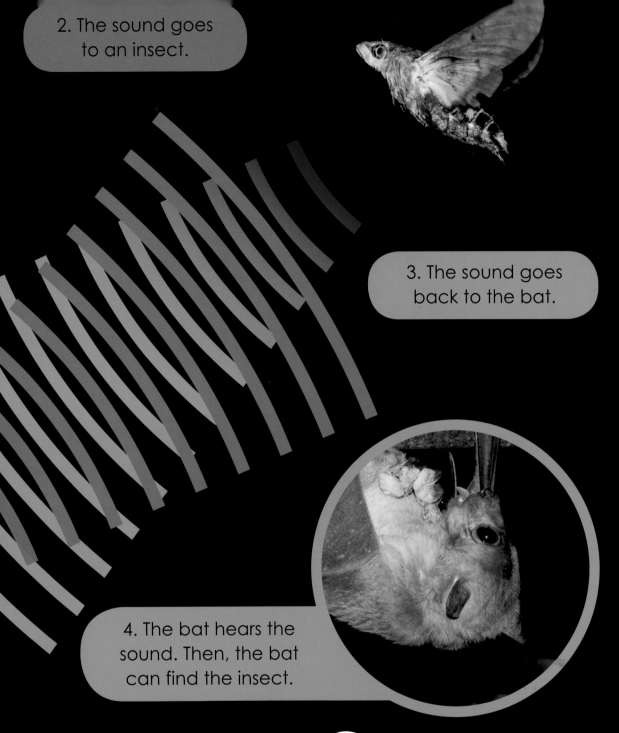

2. The sound goes to an insect.

3. The sound goes back to the bat.

4. The bat hears the sound. Then, the bat can find the insect.

LOOK!

Look at the pages.
What do bats hunt at night?

29

Quiz

Choose the correct answers.

1 A hungry wild dog . . .
   a howls.
   b sneezes.

2 A whale's sound comes
from its . . .
   a head.
   b tail.

3 Owls are . . .
   a quiet.
   b noisy.

4 Which animals laugh?
 a frogs
 b bonobos

5 Many animals hear
 with their . . .
 a feet.
 b ears.

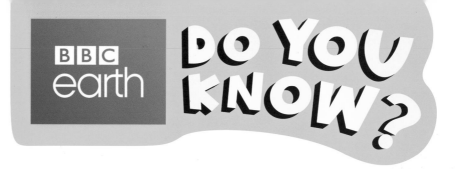

DO YOU KNOW?

Visit www.ladybirdeducation.co.uk for FREE DO YOU KNOW? teaching resources.

- video clips with simplified voiceover and subtitles
- video and comprehension activities
- class projects and lesson plans
- audio recording of every book
- digital version of every book
- full answer keys

To access video clips, audio tracks and digital books:

1 Go to **www.ladybirdeducation.co.uk**
2 Click "Unlock book"
3 Enter the code below

gKDWPm97vS

Stay safe online! Some of the DO YOU KNOW? activities ask children to do extra research online. Remember:

- ensure an adult is supervising;
- use established search engines such as Google or Kiddle;
- children should never share personal details, such as name, home or school address, telephone number or photos.